THE OTHER HANDBOOK

POWERFUL LESSONS FOR YOUR MISSION AND BEYOND

KRIS HEAP

ISBN: 978-0-9836824-8-6

Copyright © 2025 by Kris Heap

All rights reserved.

No part of this book may be reproduced in any form or by any electronic or mechanical means, including information storage and retrieval systems, without written permission from the author, except for the use of brief quotations in a book review.

ABOUT THIS BOOK

Every missionary has a similar story. It starts with a mission call, a packed suitcase, and a heart full of faith (and a little fear). And somewhere on the journey between your first awkward street contact and your final transfer, something sacred happens—you start becoming someone new.

This book is full of advice to help on that journey. It is designed so that you can read it start to finish or just pick a random page to read at any time. Wherever you land, it will be insightful.

I wrote this book just as one of my sons was about to leave on a mission to Cusco, Peru. His upcoming departure caused me to start pondering what advice I could give him that would be most helpful, not just for his next 2 years, but for his life beyond the mission. As I started writing, I began to feel the spirit of my mission returning to my heart. I opened my mission journal for the first time in 20 years and, as I read through my mission experiences, I began jotting down the life lessons I learned along the way. I then reached out to friends to ask for their best advice as well. As their suggestions came pouring in, I could feel the deep love and respect they had for you. It gave them a moment to reflect on their own missions and try to pass everything they had learned on to you in a few inspired sentences.

So what's inside isn't a checklist or a rulebook. It is a group effort to pass on the kind of wisdom you usually only learn the hard way—given by those who have walked the part of the path you are now on.

These pages were written for the elder riding his bike in the rain, the sister who feels like she's not enough, and every missionary who's ever struggled or wondered if they're making a difference.

But here's the secret...

This isn't just a missionary book. It's a *life* book. **Every single principle will still matter long after the name tag comes off.** By just changing some of the words, every principle becomes powerful for a new stage of life.

For example:

- The word "companion" can change to "spouse" or "coworker".
- The word "investigator" can change to "customer" or "sales lead".
- The word "mission" can be come "career", "school", or "calling."

So I hope you read this with your whole heart. Let it lift you when you're tired, challenge you when you're coasting, and remind you why you came on your mission in the first place. Because the Lord didn't just call you on a mission—He invited you onto a path of discipleship and transformation. Not just for today, but for a lifetime.

Kris Heap

1

THE LORD CALLED YOU TO THIS EXACT PLACE, AT THIS EXACT TIME, FOR A REASON.

You weren't sent to your mission, your zone, or your area by accident. The Lord called you to this exact place and this exact time for a reason. You need to find out why. It could be to find a specific person or learn something from this particular companion.

Don't waste energy comparing your mission to someone else's. Spiritual growth never happens in comparison, it happens when you are fully present in the situation the Lord has placed you in.

This is your soil. This is your season. Bloom right here.

Doctrine & Covenants 100:4

2

REMEMBER WHOSE NAME IS WITH YOURS ON THE BADGE.

You're not just representing the Church—you're walking with the Savior. Let that shape everything you do.

That name tag is more than plastic and ink, it's a declaration of who you are and whose side you are on. *Your* name is next to *His*. Every handshake, every doorstep, every eye that glances at your badge is a chance for someone to feel something different—not just because of your presence, but because of His.

When you remember who you're walking with, your behavior changes. There is nothing that two people can't accomplish if one of them is the Lord. Carry His name with confidence.

3 Nephi 18:24

3
ALL THINGS ARE DIFFICULT BEFORE THEY ARE EASY.

Hopefully nobody told you your mission would be easy; it won't be. It isn't supposed to be. Nothing worth doing was ever easy. The amazing views from the top of a mountain only come after the struggle to climb it.

But here's what matters most: **you can do hard things.** You are a child of God, and He walks beside you. The struggle is part of the sacred growth process. Expect it. Embrace it. And when it gets heavy, don't back down—look up. The darkest hour is just before the sun rises. Trust His plan, lean into His strength, and watch how He turns your effort into miracles.

Mosiah 24:14–15

4
FALL IN LOVE WITH THE SAVIOR. THAT WILL CHANGE EVERYTHING.

On your mission, you'll meet people who don't read, who don't show up, who don't respond. You might start to wonder if what you're doing even matters. But when you develop a love for Jesus Christ, everything changes. The mission stops being about numbers or approval or doing everything "right" —and starts being about becoming more like Him. When your heart is centered on the Savior, your teaching becomes more powerful, your prayers more thoughtful, and your patience more abundant. The love you feel for Him overflows into love for others, and that is what actually changes lives. Including your own.

1 John 4:19

5
YOU ARE WORTHY TO BE HERE.

At some point within the first days, weeks, or months of your mission, you may have the terrifying feeling that they are unworthy to be a missionary. That is a normal feeling that many experience. It is a part of the sanctifying and purifying power of the Spirit.

Jumping from your normal life into a spiritually supercharged life can be a bit of a shock. You may start to feel unworthy because of some random, minor things from your teenage years.

None of us are ever fully worthy of the Lord, that's why His grace is necessary. But as long as you have already cleared up any major issues with your bishop or stake president, you can feel confident that you are now worthy to fully serve the Lord and represent Him as a missionary.

6

LET YOUR KINDNESS DO THE TALKING.

When in doubt, just be kind.

You're not called to win arguments, you're called to win hearts to the cause of Jesus Christ. And often, the loudest message you'll preach is how you respond when people reject your invitation. Your arguments won't convert people, your *kindness will.* If they see that your love for them doesn't depend on their choices, they may one day open up. Let them remember that the missionary who knocked on their door left behind warmth, not pressure. Jesus never forced anyone to follow Him. He simply loved them, served them, taught them, and let them choose.

Proverbs 15:1

7
REMEMBER, THE LORD IS ALREADY WORKING ON PEOPLE BEFORE YOU EVER KNOCK.

You're not starting the story, you're joining it. God is already working in the hearts of His children long before you ever knock on their door or contact them on the street. Your job isn't to force faith into their life but to discover where it's already quietly blooming.

Pay attention. Ask questions. Listen closely. When you do, you'll realize that the Spirit has been there all along and you were simply invited into the moment.

Alma 16:16

8

YOU CAN'T GIVE WHAT YOU DON'T HAVE.

Before you can help someone else feel the Spirit, you need to know what it feels like yourself. Before you invite others to trust the Lord, you have to be learning to trust Him, too. Your testimony doesn't have to be perfect, but it does have to be real. Study, pray, ask questions, wrestle with your doubts—and let the gospel get deep into your bones. People can feel sincerity, and they can feel when it's missing.

You're not just teaching lessons. You're offering your heart and your light. You must carry your own fire if you want to ignite one for someone else.

D&C 11:21

9
YOU ARE STRONGER THAN YOU THINK YOU ARE.

You'll face days on your mission that test every ounce of your resolve. The homesickness, the rejections, the food, the expectations, the emotional and spiritual stretching—none of it is easy. But here's the truth: you are stronger than you think you are.

God doesn't call the most perfect people to do His work—He calls those who are willing. And in the refining fire of this experience, you'll uncover strength you didn't know you had. The Lord will magnify your efforts and the strength you need to face every challenge will be there when you need it. You are a child of God and His power is within you. Don't underestimate yourself.

Philippians 4:13

10

BE THE KIND OF COMPANION YOU'D WANT TO WORK WITH

You won't get to choose your companions, but you always get to choose who *you* are. Every missionary you're paired with is carrying burdens you may never see: homesickness, anxiety, family struggles, doubts. So lead with compassion, not comparison. Be quick to forgive, slow to judge, and generous with your kindness. You might be the one safe space they have in this time of their life.

And remember—your patience with others is also shaping you. Missionary companionships are some of God's most effective refining tools. Plus, you never know when you may need a strong companion to lift you through a hard time.

Doctrine & Covenants 18:10

11

BE INTERESTED, NOT INTERESTING.

People don't care how much you know until they know how much you care. People feel loved when they feel heard, and listening earns you the right to speak.

When you're more focused on understanding others than being understood yourself, people open up. That's when hearts soften. Good missionaries don't just teach well, they *listen well*. Ask about people's stories, their families, their doubts or struggles with life—then really listen to what they say.

When others know you genuinely care, they're more likely to trust what you say and, more importantly, Who you *represent*.

James 1:19

12

LEARN TO COOK AT LEAST THREE THINGS THAT WON'T KILL YOU OR YOUR COMPANION.

Both Ramen and revelation are both important, but only one requires a stove. Face it, sometimes your dinner appointments are going to fall through (if you're lucky enough to have them in the first place.)

Missionary life is spiritual—but it's also very physical. You can't teach with power if you're running on sugar packets and vending machine candy. Learning to cook just a few simple meals shows self-reliance, respect for your body, and care for your companion.

1 Corinthians 6:19–20

13
DON'T WAIT TO BE TOLD WHAT NEEDS TO BE DONE.

Look around. *Anticipate. Act.* Some missionaries do only what they're told. Great missionaries look for what needs doing—and do it. Whether it's straightening chairs after a meeting, starting the dishes, calling a member, or following a prompting, initiative shows love, maturity, and spiritual awareness.

You're not on the mission to be managed; you're there to minister. When you move forward with purpose, God will place people and opportunities in your path that require exactly who you are. You'll become the kind of person others can count on—and more importantly, the kind the Lord can trust.

Doctrine & Covenants 58:26-27

14
DON'T BE A TOURIST, BECOME A LOCAL.

The fastest way to open a heart is to show genuine interest in someone's world. When you take time to learn a person's culture—their food, their language quirks, their holidays, even their sports teams—you send a message: *"I am here with you and you matter to me."*

Jesus came to earth to better understand us. Follow His example. Learn to appreciate the culture you have entered. Become a Peruvian, a Texan, a Korean, or whichever place you're called to. This shows love for God's children and honors their identity. Do this, and they will love you for it.

1 Corinthians 9:22

15
"THE BEST TIME TO PLANT A TREE WAS TWENTY YEARS AGO. THE SECOND BEST TIME IS NOW."

Now that you're on your mission, this old Chinese proverb may have some meaning. You might look back and wish you'd started with more focus or built a stronger testimony before coming out. That's normal. But regret won't move you forward, action will. The best time to start becoming the missionary you want to be was yesterday. The second best time is today.

Don't wait for the next transfer or a "better area" or the "perfect companion." Start now. Plant the habits, the mindset, and the spiritual roots that will carry you the rest of your mission. You'll be glad you did.

Luke 9:62

16

IT'S OKAY NOT TO KNOW, BUT IT'S NOT OKAY TO NOT TRY.

You don't have to know everything. You don't have to be fluent, an amazing teacher, or confident in every street contact. **But you do have to try**. God doesn't expect perfection—He just asks for effort. Some of the most powerful missionary moments happen not when you say or do everything right, but when you show up with faith, humility, and a willing heart.

Don't let fear of failure become your excuse for inaction. The Spirit can work with imperfect words—but He can't steer a parked car. Just get moving and let Him take the wheel.

Proverbs 3:5-6

17
EFFORT ISN'T ONE-SIZE-FITS-ALL.

Not every companion will have the same energy, talents, or work style as you—and that's okay. What looks like 70% effort to you might actually be 100% for them. It's easy to get frustrated when you feel like you're carrying more, but choosing peace and compassion in the companionship matters more than keeping score.

Christ taught that every effort is honored and rewarded on an individual basis. That gives you permission to not judge your companion for the effort they can give. Harmony in your companionship will invite the Spirit more than any checklist ever could.

Romans 12:4–5

18

IF YOU MESS UP, OWN IT QUICKLY, FIX IT FULLY, AND MOVE ON.

Nothing earns respect faster than accountability.

You're going to mess up. You'll forget appointments, say the wrong thing, lose your temper, miss the mark. That's not the problem. The real issue is whether you'll be honest about it. Humility is magnetic—it builds trust with your companion, with your leaders, and with the Lord. The sooner you own your mistakes, the sooner grace gets to work.

The Savior isn't looking for perfect missionaries. He's looking for honest ones who are quick to repent and quick to repair. That's how trust is built and character is formed.

Doctrine & Covenants 58:43

19
WRITE DOWN SPIRITUAL IMPRESSIONS, THEN ACT ON THEM.

Keep a journal. It will become your personal scripture.

The Lord speaks in quiet ways—through thoughts, feelings, flashes of insight, and impressions that can fade if we don't capture them. When you write them down, you not only preserve them, you show the Lord that you're paying attention. That simple act of recording them becomes an invitation for more revelation.

Over time, your journal becomes a personal treasure—a testimony in your own handwriting of how God walked with you, answered your prayers, and guided your steps.

3 Nephi 23:13

20

YOU CAN'T POUR FROM AN EMPTY CUP.

You can't help others if you're running on empty. Taking care of your spiritual, emotional, and physical health isn't selfish—it's smart. Missionary work demands a lot from you, and if you're constantly giving without refilling, eventually there'll be nothing left to give.

The Savior said to "love thy neighbor *as thyself*"—not instead of yourself. That means rest when you need it. Eat well. Move your body. Stay connected through prayer and quiet time. These aren't luxuries—they're part of the job. When you stay healthy and whole, you serve with more energy, more patience, and more love. You show up not just as a missionary, but as your best self.

Mosiah 4:27

21

LEAVE PEOPLE BETTER THAN YOU FOUND THEM.

Whether it's a companion, a family, or a stranger—let their lives be warmer because of your light.

You carry more than a name tag—you carry light. Every conversation, every doorstep, every awkward first meeting is a chance to leave someone a little more seen, loved, and lifted than before. Most people won't remember your scripture references, but they'll remember how you made them feel.

At all times, especially the hard ones, strive to be kind and uplifting. That's what Jesus did. Your mission isn't just about teaching lessons; it's about *becoming one*.

3 Nephi 12:14-16

22

TREAT EVERY MISSIONARY LIKE THEY'RE YOUR SIBLING.

Missions are a training ground for lifelong relationships. Just like you didn't get to choose your siblings, you won't get to choose your companions.

But the people you serve with aren't just companions—they're family. God didn't just send you to your mission; He also sent you to *them*.

Some of your most important growth will come through those relationships—through shared struggles, successes, and connection. Celebrate their wins. Bear their burdens. Ask about their stories. The way you treat other missionaries says a lot about who you are.

John 13:35

23
BE A THERMOSTAT, NOT A THERMOMETER.

Don't just reflect the mood, elevate it.

A thermometer reflects what's around it. A thermostat *changes* what's around it. In every area, lesson, or companionship, you'll have the power to shift the spiritual climate. When people are discouraged, be the calm voice. When things are chaotic, be the peace. When negativity creeps in, be the light that pushes it out. Don't wait for someone else to lead with love, gratitude, or spiritual energy. You go first. That's what disciples do. The Savior never just reacted to His surroundings—He *transformed* them.

1 Timothy 4:12

24
SAY "THANK YOU" OFTEN AND MEAN IT.

Gratitude opens doors that no other key can unlock.

Gratitude is more than good manners—it's a spiritual superpower. It changes how you see people, how people see you, and how God responds to you. Say thank you to members who feed you, to companions who try their best, to leaders who correct you, and to strangers who give you five minutes on their porch.

A grateful heart is humble, teachable, and magnetic. The Lord can do incredible things through someone who notices His blessings and expresses gratitude for them.

Doctrine & Covenants 78:19

25
LET REJECTION BUILD YOUR RESILIENCE, NOT YOUR RESENTMENT.

Every "no" is just a step on the path to someone saying "yes."

Rejection is part of the call. Even the Savior, in His perfect love, was turned away. You're not failing when people say no. You're succeeding every time you show up, extend an invitation, and love with no expectations. Let each closed door toughen your resolve, not harden your heart. Because often, the greatest miracle comes *after* the hardest day. When you refuse to give up, you become the kind of missionary who the Lord can trust with someone He has prepared. And they *will* come.

Matthew 5:11-12

26

IF YOU FEEL THE SPIRIT LEAVE THE ROOM, PAUSE AND INVITE HIM BACK.

As a missionary, your greatest companion isn't the one sitting next to you—it's the quiet presence of the Holy Ghost. He's the teacher, the translator, the one who changes hearts. You're just the messenger.

Even with a perfectly prepared lesson or sincere intentions, if the Spirit isn't there, it's okay to stop. Take a breath. Say a prayer. Change your approach. Sometimes the most powerful thing you can do is sit in silence and wait. And if you lose that feeling for a moment, don't panic or blame yourself—just notice it, invite Him back, and move forward. He always comes where He's invited.

Doctrine & Covenants 121:46

27
BE THE REASON SOMEONE KEEPS BELIEVING IN MISSIONARIES.

Long after you're gone, people will still remember how you made them feel. Maybe they didn't accept your message—but did they feel peace when you walked in? Did they feel respected when you listened? Did they see Jesus in your actions, even if they never heard His name from your lips?

You may be just one in a long line of missionaries they meet, but you could be the one that changed the tone, healed a hurt, or reignited curiosity. *Be that kind of missionary.* Make it easy for people to believe that Christ loves them, is still calling to them, and is sending His servants to minister to them.

Alma 12:6-7

28

EAT THE WEIRD FOOD. SMILE BIG. ASK FOR SECONDS.

That's missionary work, too. Every bite is a way of saying, "I'm here with you, I respect your service and sacrifice, and I want to understand your life." People remember that kind of openness more than they remember your lesson on the Plan of Salvation. You may not realize how much of a sacrifice it was for them to put a meal together for you. It is an act of love and appreciation on their part.

When you show up with humility and joy—even at the dinner table—you make space for the Spirit to work. Good manners show respect for others. Love is in the little things, even if they don't taste the best.

Alma 17:11

29
PRAY LIKE IT ALL DEPENDS ON GOD. WORK LIKE IT ALL DEPENDS ON YOU.

When you pray, do it with your whole heart, trusting that God sees the bigger picture and will guide you to what matters most. But after the prayer, don't wait around for Him to do the work that's in your hands. Get up and get moving. Talk to strangers, follow through on promptings, lift the people around you.

The Lord often answers prayers through the people who are already working, not those who are waiting. The Lord's work isn't passive; it is collaborative.

James 2:17

30
FIND JOY IN THE SMALL AND ORDINARY.

Not every day will be thrilling—but every day can be meaningful. Most of your mission won't be spent in dramatic moments or spiritual highs. It'll be in the quiet grind of knocking doors, studying scriptures, riding bikes, washing dishes, and showing up on time. And that's okay. The Lord is present in the routine, not just in the miracles.

The Savior noticed mustard seeds, lilies, lost coins, and children. He paid attention to the ordinary because He knew that's where most of life happens. If you only look for miracles in the big and bold, you'll miss the ones unfolding right in front of you. Let the small things matter.

Alma 37:6-7

31
SUCCESS LEAVES CLUES.

When someone becomes a great missionary, it's rarely a mystery, it's a pattern. Pay attention to the elders and sisters who are thriving. What are they doing daily? How do they study? How do they treat people? How do they respond to adversity? Their success isn't accidental, it's the result of small, consistent choices.

The same is true of spiritual success. People who have powerful testimonies didn't stumble into them, they worked for them. If you want similar results, follow their example—not just to copy them, but to be inspired to develop your own faithful habits.

Philippians 3:17

32
DON'T RUSH PAST THE PEOPLE WHO JUST NEED TO BE SEEN.

Christ always stopped for the one. There will always be another appointment, another street, another task. But right in front of you may be someone who simply needs to be noticed—really noticed. A moment of eye contact, a genuine smile, or a simple "How are you doing?" can do more than an entire lesson plan.

Jesus never seemed to be in a hurry, and He always found time for the one others overlooked: the woman at the well, the blind man calling from the roadside, the child others tried to shoo away. Sometimes the most Christlike thing you can do is stop.

Luke 8:43–48

33
IF YOUR COMPANION SAYS "I THINK WE CAN MAKE IT" WHILE RIDING BIKES DOWNHILL, JUST START PRAYING.

You're about to meet Jesus . . . or the pavement.

Psalm 91:11

34
DO MORE THAN YOU'RE ASKED. EVERY TIME.

Jesus taught us not just to carry someone's pack for a mile, but for two. That second mile? That's where love lives. That's where the real growth happens. When you go above what's required—not for recognition, but because you care—you become capable of bearing greater things.

On your mission, going the extra mile might mean listening longer, praying more sincerely, or serving a companion who doesn't notice. Over time, that kind of effort becomes more than habit—it becomes who you are. And that kind of person can change the world.

Matthew 5:41

35
PRAY

When in doubt, pray. Ask for help with your area. Ask how to love your companion better. Ask for courage to speak when you're scared, or peace when you're overwhelmed. Prayer is where your weakness meets God's strength, and where your small offering becomes more than enough.

The Savior prayed before choosing His disciples, before performing miracles, and even in His deepest agony. If the Son of God needed prayer, so do we. Don't treat it like a formality. Treat it like what it is: a conversation with your Father who loves you and wants to help. He will answer.

Alma 37:36

36
WHEN THINGS GET HARD, REMEMBER: GROWTH LIVES ON THE OTHER SIDE OF DISCOMFORT.

Heavenly Father doesn't waste the pain or the struggle, He shapes His disciples with it. Discomfort is not always a sign you're doing something wrong; often, it's proof you're being stretched into someone new. Pain teaches what ease cannot. Struggle refines what comfort leaves untouched.

God doesn't send the storm to punish you, He allows it to reveal you, reshape you, and remind you whose you are. Lean in to it. Breathe. Trust in Him. He knows you and will put you in the right situations to help you grow.

Ether 12:27

37
LAUGH OFTEN, ESPECIALLY AT YOURSELF.

There's something sacred about a laugh that comes from humility. When you can chuckle at your own awkwardness or missteps, you create space for grace to enter. It softens the pressure of perfection and opens the door to connection with the Lord and those around you. A joyful heart not only lifts your spirit, it lifts others, too. Especially in hard moments, a sense of humor can remind you that you're growing and that God's still walking with you.

Christ wept, but surely He also laughed. Let yourself do both.

Proverbs 17:22

38
WHEN YOU DON'T KNOW WHAT TO SAY, JUST BEAR YOUR TESTIMONY.

Sincerity beats sophistication every time. When you feel inadequate or unsure, remember: a simple testimony, humbly shared, carries more power than the most polished lesson. People aren't looking for perfect words; they're looking for something real. Let them hear your conviction. Let them feel your faith. Your job isn't to impress people, it is to help them feel something and then invite them to act on it.

You might stammer. You might forget a verse. But if you share your testimony from your heart, the Spirit will speak to theirs.

Doctrine & Covenants 100:5–6

39
YOUR SUCCESS ISN'T MEASURED BY OUTCOMES—IT'S MEASURED BY YOUR LOVE AND EFFORT.

In missionary work, and in life, it's easy to tie your worth to numbers, goals, or visible success. But the Lord doesn't need results to love you. He's not tracking baptisms like sales goals. He's watching the quiet courage it takes to keep trying. He's shaping your character with every act of obedience, every moment of love, and every ounce of effort.

What you become in the process matters more than what you achieve. Trust that your faithful work, even when it feels unseen or unrewarded, is deeply sacred to Him.

1 Samuel 16:7

40
DON'T LET RULES BECOME YOUR RELIGION.

Rules are meant to protect your purpose, not replace it. They're scaffolding for your discipleship, not the structure itself. When rules become the center of your religion, you risk missing the very heart of the gospel—love. That's what the Pharisees did.

Obedience rooted in fear leads to burnout, comparison, and performative righteousness. But when you follow the rules out of love for the Savior and the people you're serving, your mission becomes joyful, not just dutiful.

Your mission leaders might set the standards, but it's your relationship with Christ that defines your discipleship.

John 14:15

41

IF YOU AND YOUR COMPANION BOTH WANT THE TOP BUNK, LET THE SPIRIT DECIDE.

Rock-paper-scissors is also acceptable.

Some decisions in missionary life are high-stakes—where to go, who to visit, what lesson to share. And some... are just about who gets the top bunk. But even small conflicts reveal big things about us: our willingness to yield, to laugh, and to let go of our egos.

Your companionship is a classroom where you're learning to live with someone else. Sometimes that means praying about important things. Sometimes it means flipping a coin.

The top bunk isn't eternal. But how you treat your companion might just shape your eternity.

Philippians 2:3

42

BE FLUENT IN THREE LANGUAGES: YOUR MISSION LANGUAGE, KINDNESS, AND SILENCE.

There is a time for each. Language study may be part of your daily schedule, but some of the most powerful languages are never written in a textbook. Kindness speaks when words fail. Silence speaks when the Spirit needs some space to work. Being fluent in the unwritten languages can open more hearts than a perfect discussion ever could.

Learn to read the room. Sometimes the person in front of you doesn't need a scripture, they need a smile. Other times, the Spirit is trying to speak and just needs you to stop talking.

Ecclesiastes 3:7

43
YOU BECOME WHAT YOU REPEATEDLY DO.

Your habits are forming your future. All of the small, repeated actions you do every day are shaping the missionary you're becoming. You're not just checking boxes; you're becoming someone. And who you become matters more than what you accomplish.

Consistency builds character. It doesn't matter if today feels boring or slow. What matters is showing up with integrity, again and again. Because the kind of missionary the Lord can trust isn't made in a moment, it's made in a thousand quiet, faithful ones. You don't rise to the level of your goals, you fall to the level of your habits.

Doctrine and Covenants 130:18–19

44
NOT EVERY DAY IS A MOUNTAINTOP. SOME ARE MUSTARD SEED DAYS.

Missionary work isn't all spiritual fireworks and golden investigators. Some days are slow. Some feel unremarkable. But just because it's not a "miracle" day doesn't mean it's not sacred. The small acts like offering a prayer, smiling at a stranger, or showing up when you're tired are mustard seeds. You won't always see what they become, but the Lord does.

Keep planting kindness. Keep scattering hope. Even when it feels like nothing is happening, the Lord is watching, watering, and waiting.

Keep planting. You'll be amazed at what grows later.

Doctrine & Covenants 64:33

45
BE SOMEONE THE LORD CAN TRUST IN ANY HOUSE, ON ANY STREET, IN ANY CONVERSATION.

Character is who you are when nobody's watching. Integrity isn't just a missionary attribute; it's a divine quality. God isn't looking for performers, He's looking for disciples—people He can trust to represent Him in both quiet corners and crowded avenues.

The world often rewards appearances, but the Lord rewards substance. He sees your heart. He knows your intentions. And He notices the moments you choose honesty and humility, even when no one else does.

Psalm 15:1–2

46
SEEK PROGRESS, NOT PERFECTION.

The Lord asks for your heart, not a flawless track record.

Obedience is important. But perfection as a missionary? That's never been the requirement nor is it even possible. You will mess up. You'll oversleep, forget a commitment, say the wrong thing. That doesn't make you unworthy, it makes you human. The Lord knows that.

The goal isn't flawlessness; the goal is progress. Try to be a little better every day. Real obedience is about love, not fear. It's about saying, "Here I am, Lord. I'm trying." He can work with that. He rejoices in every effort you make.

Moroni 10:32

47
IF YOU THINK YOU DON'T NEED DEODORANT—YOU'RE WRONG.

Hygiene is not just about courtesy; it's about stewardship. You represent Christ in all things—your words, your service, your appearance, and yes, even your scent. Respect yourself. Respect your companion. Anoint thyself... with Speed Stick.

1 Corinthians 6:19–20

48

WHEN IN DOUBT, TAKE OUT THE TRASH, WASH THE DISHES, AND SAY A PRAYER.

There will be times of tension in your companionships. Sometimes, the most spiritual thing you can do is scrub a pan, polish some shoes, or sweep a floor. Why? Because small acts of service restore peace. They break down walls. They remind both you and your companion who you really are: servants of Christ.

When frustration sets in, don't wait for someone else to change. Your hands can offer an apology even before your mouth does. And your knees, bent in prayer, can open doors no conversation ever could.

John 13:14–15

49
DON'T TRY TO WIN ARGUMENTS.

Love is more persuasive than logic. You will never convert or convince someone through an argument, and people don't open their hearts because they lost a debate. They open their hearts when they feel heard, validated, and loved. Doctrine has power, yes, but it is love that unlocks the door.

Jesus didn't argue people into discipleship; He walked with them, wept with them, healed them. Your job isn't to prove you're right, it's to prove you care. Remember, the Spirit is not sent to confirm your cleverness but to confirm the truth spoken in love.

Doctrine and Covenants 121:41–42

50
IF YOU'RE FEELING DISCOURAGED, REREAD YOUR MISSION CALL.

Some days feel heavier than others. You might question your ability, your purpose, or even your place in this calling to serve. On those days, pull out that letter, not because the words have changed, but because *you* need to remember who wrote them.

You were not chosen by accident or default. The Lord knew exactly what would unfold—your strengths, your fears, your imperfections—and still said: "Yes, I want *this* one."

When you forget your worth, let those words remind you: *You are called of God. And He does not un-choose His children.*

Alma 26:27

51
BE THE MISSIONARY THAT YOUR TEN-YEAR-OLD-SELF THOUGHT YOU WOULD BE.

This is the adventure you looked forward to, make it count.

Before you had a name tag or a companion, before you learned a language or memorized the scripture verses, there was a younger version of you who dreamed of this. Maybe they didn't know all the rules, the exhaustion, or the rejection—but they knew they wanted to serve in the Lords' army.

You're living the dream your younger self once prayed for. So live it fully. Live it faithfully. And when it's all over, imagine that 10-year-old giving you a high-five.

Ether 12:4

52
LEARN TO LOVE THE WIDOWED MEMBER AS MUCH AS THE GOLDEN INVESTIGATOR.

It's easy to get excited about the person who's ready to say yes—who's reading the Book of Mormon, coming to church, asking for a baptism date. But don't overlook the quiet widow who just needs someone to listen. She may not change your stats, but she might just change your heart.

Some people are searching for truth, others are just searching for someone who acknowledges them. You're not here to decide which deserves your attention, you're here to love everyone. Because in God's eyes there are no "golden contacts"—they are all His children.

Doctrine & Covenants 18:10

53
A GOOD MISSIONARY IS ONE WHO MAKES IT EASY FOR PEOPLE TO BELIEVE IN GOD AGAIN.

Many people you'll meet aren't looking for more doctrine—they're struggling to believe that God knows them. They need to see what grace looks like in real time. A missionary who is calm, present, sincere, and nonjudgmental can reopen hearts that have been closed for years.

You don't have to be the reason someone joins the Church. But you can be the reason they believe God's love is still possible. That maybe, just maybe, God hasn't given up on them. If you can bring them that hope, they will open their heart.

Alma 5:14

54
A SMOOTH SEA NEVER MADE A SKILLED SAILOR.

Easy days don't make great missionaries—hard ones do. The setbacks, the slammed doors, the lessons that fall apart, the companions who challenge your patience—these are your storms. But they are also your training ground.

The Savior doesn't just want you to get through your mission, He wants to shape you through it. Every wave you face refines your faith, stretches your heart, and deepens your dependence on Him. You're not being punished by the rough seas, you're being prepared. The most seasoned sailors are forged in storms and so are the most faithful disciples.

Doctrine & Covenants 122:7

55
DON'T LET ANYONE ELSE'S BAD ATTITUDE STEAL YOUR JOY.

You get to choose what kind of missionary you'll be every single day. Some days, your companion might be grumpy. The people you meet might be rude. The work might feel slow. But your attitude? That's your sacred ground. Guard it. Don't give others the power to decide your mood, your mindset, or your mission.

Joy is a fruit of the Spirit—not the product of easy circumstances. You get to choose light and positivity again and again no matter what is going on around you.

2 Nephi 2:27

56
"DON'T BE AN IDIOT."

That's the phrase a local teacher tells her incoming junior high students at the start of each school year.

You're in your late teens to early 20's, and your prefrontal cortex won't fully form until you're 25. The prefrontal cortex is the part of your brain that acts like the brakes. It's the part that says, "Maybe I shouldn't do that, there could be some negative consequences to that choice."

Since your prefrontal cortex isn't fully formed yet, you will have to rely on the Spirit—that still small voice that says something like, "Hey, don't be an idiot. This is a bad idea." The best missionary in the world is useless if they're at home getting surgery because of an injury sustained doing something dumb or dangerous.

57
WHEN YOU FALL SHORT (AND YOU WILL), REPENT QUICKLY AND KEEP WALKING.

You're going to fall short. You're going to mess up and make a bad decision. That's not a prophecy, it's a promise.

But failure doesn't disqualify you from discipleship. When it happens, repent quickly. Don't sit in shame or rehearse your mistakes, that's not what the Lord asks of you. His grace is like a river, not a stagnant pond. Let it carry you forward.

Repentance is learning combined with a change of heart. It is not meant to be a punishment but an opportunity. So get back up, take the next step, and keep serving. That's what having faith in the Savior and His atonement looks like.

2 Corinthians 12:9

58
YOU'LL COME HOME WITH SOUVENIRS, LANGUAGE SKILLS, AND STORIES—BUT YOUR GREATEST TREASURE WILL BE WHO YOU BECAME.

Let the Lord work on you while you work for Him. Missions are less about changing the world and more about letting Christ change you.

As you contact people and teach lessons, you're also being taught—about humility, grace, patience, and love. God doesn't just call you to serve; He calls you to become something more than you were when you began your mission. And if you let Him, He will use every moment to shape you into someone more like Him.

Philippians 1:6

59
DON'T JUST STUDY PREACH MY GOSPEL— LIVE IT.

It's more than a manual or checklist; it's a pattern for becoming a better disciple of Jesus Christ for your entire life. As you live its principles with real intent, you begin to embody the very message you're sharing. You become more than a teacher, you become a true disciple. Let the power of Preach My Gospel work in you, until Christ's image begins to shine in your countenance.

Doctrine and Covenants 11:21
Alma 5:14

60

WHEN YOU FEEL INADEQUATE, REMEMBER THIS: GOD DOESN'T CALL THE MOST QUALIFIED—HE QUALIFIES THOSE WHO HE CALLS.

When you feel inadequate (and you will), remember that God never expected perfection—He expected willingness. You were set apart not because you had it all figured out, but because He saw who you could become.

God has never called a prophet that was already super-qualified to be a prophet. He called them as they were, and helped them grow into their calling.

He will do the same for you. You are not alone in this work.

Jeremiah 1:5

61

GOD'S PLAN PROBABLY DOESN'T INVOLVE YOU ARGUING ON SOMEONE'S DOORSTEP.

Convincing someone through a loud voice or clever argument was never the Savior's way—and it shouldn't be yours either.

If the Spirit leaves the conversation, you probably should too.

God's plan unfolds through love, not debate. A soft answer is more powerful than any well-rehearsed monologue. Let your tone invite the Spirit as much as your words do. After all, it's not your job to win arguments—it's your calling to win hearts.

2 Timothy 2:24–25
Doctrine & Covenants 121:41–42

62

LAUGH WITH YOUR COMPANION EVERY DAY. ESPECIALLY WHEN EVERYTHING GOES WRONG.

That's how lifelong friendships are forged. The lesson falls through, the bus breaks down, your shoes get soaked—and somehow, the only thing left to do is laugh. These are the moments that weld two people together, not just as fellow missionaries, but as lifelong friends. Joy is a form of resilience. When you laugh, you're saying, "This won't break me. We're still in this." The Lord didn't just send you out alone—He gave you someone to walk beside, to carry the load, and to help you find light even in the long days.

Proverbs 17:22

63
NEVER TRUST A COMPANION WHO SAYS, "I THINK I REMEMBER HOW TO GET THERE."

Pack snacks, you're about to discover a new area. Just remember: detours make the best memories. Mission life is as much about the journey as the destination. Whether you're truly lost or just taking the scenic route, the Lord can use even wrong turns to lead you somewhere important—maybe even to someone who needs you. And if nothing else, you'll have a good story and a closer bond by the end of it.

Proverbs 3:5–6

64
IT DOESN'T MATTER HOW SLOW YOU GO AS LONG AS YOU DON'T STOP.

It doesn't matter how slow you go—as long as you don't stop. Some days you'll teach with power. Other days, just getting out the door will feel like a win. That's okay. The Lord isn't focused on speed—He's looking for consistency.

Faithfulness isn't about sprinting; it's about staying on the path, even when you're tired, discouraged, or unsure. Just keep going. Keep praying. Keep studying. Keep loving. The Lord isn't looking for perfect missionaries, He's looking for consistent ones. If you just keep on walking, one day you'll look up and realize just how far you've come.

Doctrine & Covenants 123:17

65
THINK ABOUT YOUR INVESTIGATORS' REAL CONCERNS.

Before you teach a commandment, take time to understand a concern. An investigator worried about feeding their kids may not be ready to talk about giving up coffee. Someone overwhelmed with work or parenting might be more in need of a listening ear than a lesson plan. Remember: you are not just delivering a message—you are meeting one of God's children. Don't rush past their real-life struggles to check off a teaching box. Christ never ignored someone's pain just to share a principle—He met their needs first, and then invited them to follow Him.

Mosiah 18:8–9

66

ASK FOR HELP.

You don't earn spiritual points by pretending everything's fine. The mission is hard—emotionally, mentally, and spiritually—and that's exactly why you were never meant to do it alone. Ask for help. From your companion, your mission leaders, your family, your Father in Heaven.

Don't suffer in silence when healing could begin with a conversation. Even Jesus, in Gethsemane, didn't walk alone—He brought His friends and cried out to the Father. You can, too.

Matthew 26:37–39

67
TAKE PICTURES OF PEOPLE, NOT JUST PLACES.

It's easy to fill your camera roll with cathedrals, sunsets, and scenic alleyways—but those aren't the moments that will stay with you. Years from now, it won't be the buildings or landscapes you'll want to see again, it'll be the face of the brother who showed up to every lesson, the sister who fed you every Sunday, or the companion who helped you laugh through the hardest times of your mission.

The buildings won't remember you, but the people will. And you'll want to remember them too. One day, those faces will bring the Spirit back into your heart in ways no postcard photo ever could.

Alma 17:2

68

TRY TO BE TAUGHT AS MUCH AS YOU TEACH.

If you show up thinking you're the only one with truth to give, you'll miss half the miracles. Every home you enter, every person you meet, carries a story that can teach you something. It could be about resilience, humility, faith, or love.

The Lord didn't just call you to speak; He called you to listen. He didn't just send you to teach others; He sent you to be changed by them. Approach your mission with a student's heart, not just a teacher's voice. The more you're willing to learn, the more power your message will carry.

Doctrine and Covenants 1:26

69
LEARN SOMETHING NEW EVERY DAY

Growth doesn't come in giant leaps, it comes in daily steps. Commit to learning something new every single day of your mission. It might be a new word in your language, a scripture to use during a lesson, a cultural insight, or something meaningful about your companion.

Little by little, line upon line, those small moments of learning add up to transformation. And with each step forward, you'll feel the joy and confidence that come from becoming more of who God created you to be.

It's not about being the best, it's about being better than you were yesterday.

2 Nephi 28:30

70
RECORD YOUR FEELINGS AS MUCH AS YOUR ACTIONS.

Your mission journal isn't just a travel log—it's a treasure chest. Don't just write what you did; write how it felt. Where did you see God show up that day? What made you laugh? What broke your heart? What grew your faith? These are the threads that will one day bind your story to someone else's.

Long after the names and dates fade, the feelings will remain. Write for your future self. Write for your children. Write for the one person who may need your story someday to lift them up and believe that God is still in the details.

2 Nephi 4:15–16

71
DON'T BE "THAT GUY".

Don't waste your energy always looking for loopholes or bending the rules. The standards you've been given aren't barriers—they're bridges to spiritual power, unity, and protection.

Yes, it might feel thrilling to push the edges, but over time, that habit chips away at your integrity. And when a moment comes that really matters—when someone needs your full strength, your full obedience, your full heart—you'll wish you'd built the kind of character that could carry it. Be steady. Be someone your companion, your mission president, and the Lord can count on.

Mosiah 27:8–10

72
DON'T BE THE OTHER KIND OF "THAT GUY".

You know the one—always correcting everyone else, quoting the handbook like it's scripture, or thinking he's more righteous than the rest of the district. There's a fine line between being obedient and being obnoxious. Mission life is better when you lead by example with humility, not superiority.

Be the elder or sister people trust, not the one they avoid. The best missionaries don't make it about themselves—they lift others, laugh at themselves, and point people to Christ, not to their own example.

Luke 18:11–14

73
WHEN IN DOUBT, GO OUT AND WORK.

There will be days when nothing makes sense—your lessons fall through, your companion's in a mood, and you start wondering if you're even making a difference. Sometimes you won't even feel like leaving your apartment. That's when the best answer is usually the simplest one: lace up your shoes and go out to work anyway. The Lord honors action. Action invites revelation. The answers you're praying for often come while you're already in motion. If you're feeling stuck, you need to push your self to change your position or location. Just start moving in the right direction and you'll feel better in no time.

Doctrine & Covenants 58:27

74
IF SOMEONE OFFERS YOU FOOD AND SAYS "IT'S A DELICACY," BRACE YOURSELF.

It's either something sacred or still moving. Either way, you're in for a story. Part of missionary work is stepping into someone else's world—even if that means chewing cautiously while pretending you're fine. The hospitality of others is sacred, and receiving it with humility is part of your discipleship.

So bless it, taste it, and trust that your stomach—and the Spirit—can handle more than you think.

Seriously though, even if you bless it, remember to have some medicine back at the apartment. Faith without Pepto is dead.

1 Corinthians 10:31

75
WHEN YOU'RE EARLY, YOU'RE ON TIME. WHEN YOU'RE ON TIME, YOU'RE LATE. WHEN YOU'RE LATE, YOU'RE LOST.

Missionary life runs on timing. From lessons to district meetings to daily planning, your willingness to be prompt shows your respect—not just for rules, but for people and for the Lord. Being early shows others that you are committed to this work in your heart. It shows that you're engaged, not just checking boxes.

When you're prepared and present, the Spirit has room to work. But when you're always rushing, distracted, or apologizing for being late, you miss opportunities to minister with peace.

Mosiah 4:27

76
THE HARDER YOU WORK, THE LUCKIER YOU GET.

Some missionaries seem to always be in the right place at the right time. They find the golden contacts. Their investigators show up to church. Everything seems to click. It might look like luck, but more often, it's just the natural result of consistent, dedicated effort.

When you're working hard—studying deeply, listening to the Spirit, making the extra contacts—you create more opportunities for miracles to happen. The Lord magnifies our efforts. "Lucky" missionaries usually aren't lucky, they're just always working. And when the Lord is looking for someone to bless, it makes sense to send those blessings to someone already moving their feet.

Doctrine and Covenants 58:27

77
PERSECUTION BINDS YOU TO THE SAVIOR.

When you face rejection, mockery, or even hostility for your beliefs, don't let it harden your heart—let it draw you closer to Christ. He walked this road before you, and every step of persecution you take in His name becomes sacred ground. These are the moments when discipleship stops being theory and becomes real.

If people misunderstand you, misjudge you, or mistreat you, remember: they did the same to Him. And He promised, *"Blessed are ye when men shall revile you...for great is your reward in heaven."* You're not alone—you're walking with Him.

3 Nephi 12:10–12

78
FIND YOUR STORY IN THE SCRIPTURES.

You are not the first to feel inadequate, exhausted, homesick, or unsure of your purpose. The scriptures are filled with people just like you—ordinary disciples who did extraordinary things in the Lord's service.

When you study the stories of Alma the Younger, Ammon, David, Esther, Nephi, or Peter, don't just read their lives—look for your reflection in them. Their fears, faith, and failures will start to feel familiar. Their courage will feel contagious. When you find your story in the scriptures, you'll find strength to write your own with more trust, more heart, and more hope.

Romans 15:4

79
BE THE KIND YOU CAN COUNT ON.

Be the kind of missionary others can count on—especially when no one is watching. There may come a time when you're serving in a remote area, far from mission leadership and fellow missionaries. In those moments, your character matters most. Be the kind of missionary who does the right thing, not for recognition, but because it's who you are. Your mission leaders are looking for someone trustworthy, steady, and spiritually mature. More importantly, the Lord is always looking for someone He can send anywhere—someone who will be faithful in all circumstances. Be that kind of missionary. Be the one He can trust.

Alma 53:20–21

80

DON'T WASTE THE PHONE CALL HOME.

Call your mom. It may sound simple, but it's crucial. Your weekly chance to talk with family is more than a catch-up session—it's part of your ministry. Use those moments to share your experiences, testify of what the Lord is doing in your life, and express gratitude. Your words can strengthen the faith of your parents, siblings, and extended family. Sometimes the most powerful missionary work you do won't be with strangers, it'll be with those who already love you. Don't take that call for granted. Use it to uplift and bless your home even when you're far away.

3 John 1:4

81

EVERY MISSION IS A SERVICE MISSION.

When all else fails and you can't find people to teach, go find people to serve. Rake a yard, carry groceries, paint a fence, or volunteer at a food bank. The Lord's work isn't limited to lessons—it's found in love. Service softens hearts, including your own, and often opens doors that preaching alone cannot.

When people see you quietly helping, they'll wonder who you are and why you care. That's your moment to testify, not just with words, but with your actions. When done right, every mission is a service mission.

Mosiah 2:17

82

DO IT ANYWAY.

Some days you are going to feel too tired to go out in the morning, or too nervous to approach a stranger on the street—even when the Spirit prompts you to. **Do it anyway.** Not because you feel brave or energized, but because you said yes to the Lord's call.

Sometimes discipleship looks like showing up with shaky knees and a quiet prayer in your heart. But those are often the days when miracles unfold, not because you were strong, but because you were willing. The Lord does some of His best work through tired, trembling hands. So take the step. Open your mouth. Trust that the Lord will meet you there.

2 Timothy 1:7

83
NO GOOD EFFORT IS EVER WASTED.

It's not about being perfect, it's about being available. You might stumble over your language. You might forget a scripture or sweat through your shirt. But if you show up with a willing heart and obedient spirit, the Lord can work wonders through you. He doesn't need perfect, He needs missionaries who will say, "Here I am. Send me," even when they feel weak, flawed, or unsure.

The Lord takes our efforts, no matter how small they seem, and turns them into something beautiful. So don't hold back because you're not "ready enough." The Lord delights in using imperfect instruments to play divine music.

Isaiah 6:8

84

LEADERSHIP IS ABOUT SERVICE—NOT STATUS

On your mission, you might be called to lead—perhaps as a district leader, zone leader, or trainer. But leadership in the Lord's kingdom isn't about prestige or being in charge. It's about lifting others rather than elevating yourself. The best leaders are those who care more about people than position.

True leadership means being the first to act, the first to listen, and often, the last to be recognized. Jesus showed us the pattern: He knelt and washed feet. He bore others' burdens. He gave everything. If you want to lead like Him, serve the way He did. Leadership is an opportunity to serve on a greater scale.

Matthew 23:11

85
ASSUME THE BEST. IGNORE THE WORST.

Your companion isn't trying to ruin your mission. And the people you're teaching aren't waking up in the morning thinking, "How can I disappoint the missionaries today?" Everyone you meet is carrying more than you can see. That quiet companion might be dealing with anxiety. That friend who won't commit might be holding back because of fear, trauma, or family pressure. You're stepping into people's lives mid-sentence—don't pretend you know the whole story.

So take a breath, soften your heart, and remember: everyone's fighting battles you can't see. Be the one to make the fight a little lighter.

Matthew 7:1-2

86

BE MORE INTERESTED IN PEOPLE THAN IN STATISTICS.

Every person you meet is a child of God—not a project, not a number, not a checkbox. If someone doesn't accept your invitation, that doesn't mean the time was wasted. Love them anyway. Honor their agency. Bear witness with gentleness.

The Savior didn't teach in order to tally conversions. He loved, healed, wept, and walked with people who often never followed Him. That same Christ walks with you. And if your mission becomes more about compassion than counting, you'll have served like He did.

Luke 15:4-7

87
SERVE THOSE YOU STRUGGLE WITH MOST.

When tension runs high in a companionship or personalities just don't click, the best way forward isn't avoidance—it's service. Real, heartfelt service. Not the kind you do to prove a point, but the kind that opens your heart. Start small if you need to. A sincere compliment like, "Hey, I like that tie," can be the first crack in a thick wall.

When you look for ways to serve them, something inside you starts to shift. You begin to see them differently, tension gives way to trust, walls start to come down, and what once felt impossible becomes new ground for connection and understanding.

Romans 12:10

88

YOUR WAY ISN'T THE ONLY WAY

If you're lucky, you'll have companions from all over the world who will quietly teach you the beauty of diversity. You'll see faith expressed in different tones, prayers offered with different accents, and hospitality shared through different customs. As you serve with them, you'll realize that God speaks every language—and not just with words.

So be curious. Be humble. Be teachable. The gospel isn't about creating sameness, it's about creating Zion, a place where all are one in heart, even when their traditions are different. The more you stop trying to make others like you, the more room you'll have to start loving them.

Acts 10:34-35

89
PUT THE "LAW OF THE HARVEST" TO WORK FOR YOU.

The Law of the Harvest is simple: *you reap what you sow*. Every effort you give plants a seed—and those seeds grow. If you approach your mission with diligence, sincerity, and love, results will come. Maybe not all at once, and maybe not as you expect, but they will come. But don't forget—the soil doesn't lie. If you plant laziness, negativity, or contention, you can't expect a harvest of miracles. You get out what you put in. Always.

So what are you planting; not just in your area, but in your heart? The harvest always comes. So make sure what grows is something you're proud of.

Doctrine and Covenants 6:33

90
AND IT CAME TO PASS...

That's more than just a scriptural phrase, it's a spiritual truth. Nothing in the mission lasts forever. The hard companions, the golden investigators, the slow weeks, the miracle baptisms—they all *come to pass*, not to stay. That's the nature of this sacred, stretching work.

So hold the highs with deep gratitude, knowing they are gifts. And face the lows with quiet faith, knowing they are temporary. The joy won't last forever, but neither will the struggle. Learn to be present for all of it. Let it pass *through* you, shape you, and then move on.

Mosiah 24:15–16

91
THE BEST LESSON PLANS INCLUDE: A STORY, A QUESTION, A SCRIPTURE, AND A MOMENT OF SILENCE.

You don't need flashy object lessons or perfectly timed jokes to teach with power. What people remember, what pierces their heart, is the Spirit. And it doesn't shout. It comes in the spaces between your words, when someone is thinking about their own life, and when the Lord has room to whisper to them.

A story opens the heart. A question invites contemplation. A scripture anchors it in truth. A moment of silence lets the Spirit speak. Let your lesson be more than information. Let it become an invitation.

3 Nephi 17:3

92
DON'T OVERSTAY YOUR WELCOME.

Many people will open their homes and hearts to you as a missionary—treat that kindness with deep respect. Be warm, be grateful, and share your message with sincerity, but be mindful of people's time and space. The Spirit often leaves quietly, and so should you.

Lingering too long can shift the feeling from inspired to intrusive. Leave them wanting more of the gospel, not less of your company. Honor their hospitality by showing good boundaries and even better gratitude.

Proverbs 25:17

93
MAKE IT IMPORTANT

It's good to be chill. It keeps you steady when things get stressful. But don't let a laid-back personality become an excuse for apathy. Missionary work matters. Souls matter. The people you're serving aren't just another name on the planner—they're children of God in need of hope, healing, and truth. That requires urgency. It doesn't mean rushing or being frantic; it means waking up each day with purpose in your step and fire in your heart.

The work of the Lord deserves your energy, focus, and best effort. Don't treat it like a side project. Speak like it matters. Study like it matters. Serve like it matters—because it does.

Jacob 5:72

94
DON'T QUIT JUST BEFORE THE BLESSINGS COME.

The Law of the Harvest says that you shall reap what you sow. The trick is that you don't know exactly when the harvest will come. Some people plant the right seeds and labor for a period of time, but then abandon the field entirely just before the crops start to grow.

If you've planted seeds with faith, don't abandon everything because you're tired or discouraged. Stay faithful. Keep showing up. Trust that your obedience is doing more than you can see. Often, the greatest blessings come just after the hardest trials. Hold on a little longer—you might be closer than you think.

Galatians 6:7-9

95
EAT THE FROG.

Mark Twain said, "If it's your job to eat a frog, it's best to do it first thing in the morning." In other words, tackle the thing you least want to do right away—don't let it loom over your whole day. Whether it's cleaning your apartment or making a tough phone call, putting it off just prolongs the dread. Get it done early, and the rest of your day will feel lighter and more productive.

After all, if you really had to eat a frog, would you want to torture yourself by sitting there looking at it all day?

Proverbs 6:6-8

96
BE AN INVESTIGATOR

Your mission is a time to not only teach, but to also be an investigator. Study the gospel, immerse yourself in the scriptures, and look for the Lord's hand in everything you do.

And don't overlook one of your most important learning opportunities: your companion. They are not just your partner in the work—they are a person with stories, hopes, struggles, and strength. Ask about their life before the mission. Listen to their dreams for the future. The more you understand them, the more unified you'll become and the more powerfully the Spirit will work through you both.

John 7:17
Mosiah 18:21

97
HAVE A TALK READY TO GO.

You will have many opportunities to give a talk while on your mission. Many of those opportunities may be impromptu. If a speaker cancels last minute or the bishop needs someone to fill extra time, chances are you will be asked to help.

Take time early in your mission to write out a message that reflects your testimony, your favorite scriptures, and a personal experience or two. Keep it in your scriptures or planner. Having a talk ready isn't just about being organized—it's about being willing and able when the Lord calls on you.

1 Peter 3:15

98
HOW YOU DO ANYTHING IS HOW YOU DO EVERYTHING.

I once had a mission leader use this phrase: **"So goes your mission, so goes your life."** He was saying that if you worked hard and effectively on your mission, you would probably do the same in your life when you got home. But if you were a slacker on the mission, you would likely be a slacker in your post-mission life.

Maybe that's true and maybe it isn't. But I do know that your mission is the time to develop the habit of giving your best effort at everything you do. If you form that habit as a missionary, you will probably carry it into those crucial few years after you get home.

Strive to do the little things well and you will most likely do everything well.

99
THE MAN WHO MOVES A MOUNTAIN BEGINS BY CARRYING AWAY SMALL STONES.

Big goals can feel overwhelming: learning a new language, understanding the scriptures deeply, finding and teaching someone prepared for baptism. But lasting success doesn't come from one dramatic act, it comes from thousands of small, faithful ones. The missionary who sees miracles is usually the one who showed up every day, even when nothing seemed to be happening.

The man who moves a mountain begins by carrying away small stones. So carry today's stone. Study a verse. Knock one more door. Be kind to your companion. Say one more prayer. All of those little acts add up to something amazing.

Alma 37:6-7

100

YOU CAN'T CONTROL THE WIND, BUT YOU CAN ADJUST YOUR SAILS.

Some days will feel like smooth sailing: appointments hold, people are receptive, your companion feels like a best friend. Other days, the wind shifts: people cancel, you feel homesick, the language isn't clicking, and nothing seems to go right.

You can't always control those winds. But you can adjust your sails. That means choosing your attitude, your effort, and your focus—especially when circumstances are outside your control. Adaptability is one of the greatest spiritual tools you'll develop. The Lord rarely promises calm seas, but He does promise to guide all who keep sailing toward Him.

1 Nephi 18:8-23

101

YOU DON'T RISE TO THE LEVEL OF YOUR GOALS— YOU FALL TO THE LEVEL OF YOUR HABITS.

You'll set goals often on your mission— how many people you want to teach, how many will come to church, or how many will enter the waters of baptism. Goals matter because they give you direction. They help you aim higher, stretch your faith, and focus your energy.

But setting a goal alone won't change anything. What creates success is what happens next. Goals are only as powerful as the habits they inspire. If your goal is to teach more people, then you might need to study more deeply, speak up more boldly, or listen more closely to the Spirit. When the initial motivation fades—and it will—it's your daily discipline that makes the difference.

102

IF YOU WANT TO GO FAST, GO ALONE. IF YOU WANT TO GO FAR, GO TOGETHER.

Sometimes you may be tempted to try and do it all yourself. Maybe you have a less-experienced companion or are serving in a small branch with a ward mission leader who was just baptized 3 months ago. You may think to yourself, "If I want it done right, I have to do it myself."

It is important to remember that the Lord works through group projects. When He sent His disciples, He sent them two by two—not because it was easier, but because it was better. You're not just called to be a missionary; you're called to be a companion, a teammate, and a builder of Zion. And Zion is always a group project.

Moses 7:18

103
BE YOUR OWN BEST HYPE-MAN (OR WOMAN)

Missionary work is full of highs and lows. Sometimes you'll feel like you're not doing good enough. In those moments, how you talk to yourself matters. You'd never tear down a struggling companion—so don't do it to yourself.

Be patient with yourself. Encourage yourself like you would a friend. The conversation in your head can either drain you or sustain you.

If it is hard for you to talk positively to yourself, try this: think of your favorite image of the Savior and imagine what He would say to you or about you. I promise it would be nothing but love and encouragement.

That is how you should talk to yourself and the type of voice you should listen to.

104
WHEN THE DOOR DOESN'T OPEN, TRY A WINDOW.

Missionary work isn't one-size-fits-all. If traditional approaches like knocking doors aren't working, it's okay to get creative. The Spirit is innovative—let your methods reflect that.

Host a free English or family history class. Join a local clean-up or community event. Use your talents like music, sports, art, or service to build real connections. Let your unique personality become a part of your ministry.

The key is love. If your goal is to lift others and bring them to Christ, there's room to try new things. Be bold. Be thoughtful. Be yourself. Be creative—and let the Lord guide the rest.

Matthew 10:16

105
HARD CHOICES, EASY LIFE. EASY CHOICES, HARD LIFE.

The mission teaches you that the most meaningful things rarely come easy. Waking up early, pushing through rejection, choosing to study when you're exhausted—these are hard choices. But over time, they create a life filled with purpose, confidence, and spiritual strength. Easy choices like cutting corners, sleeping in, or avoiding hard conversations might feel good in the moment, but they lead to regret, guilt, and stagnation. Discipline now leads to freedom later.

The Lord isn't asking for perfection. He's asking for your honest, consistent effort. Because He knows that the path to peace is usually uphill.

Hebrews 12:11

106

TIME FLIES, DON'T WASTE IT.

Your mission is just a blink in the timeline of your life, but it can shape who you become forever. Don't waste it by coasting or counting down. You'll never get this time back. Give it everything. Work hard. Love deeply. Serve fully. Come home tired not because you slacked off, but because you left every ounce of your energy in the field.

Regret is a heavy burden—faithful effort never is. You can rest later. Right now, give God your best.

Doctrine and Covenants 4:2

107
GROW THROUGH WHAT YOU GO THROUGH.

Not everything that's hard is bad. On your mission, you'll face rejection, loneliness, language barriers, and unexpected trials. But these aren't detours from your growth—they *are* your growth. The Lord doesn't waste anything you go through. He uses it to shape you into someone stronger, wiser, and more compassionate than you were before.

Trials aren't roadblocks—they're building blocks. You might not always see the growth in the moment, but if you keep going, you'll eventually look back and realize how much you've changed.

Romans 5:3-4

108

SEE THE BIG PICTURE.

It's easy to get tunnel vision in the mission field. You start measuring success by the number of lessons taught, commitments kept, or doors slammed in your face. But remember: God is playing the long game. You are planting seeds that may not bloom until years from now. You may never see the fruits—but you are part of something eternal. Don't let daily disappointments shrink your vision. Lift your eyes. You're not just serving a mission—you're shaping a soul. And that soul is yours.

2 Corinthians 4:17–18

109
"MAN DOES NOT LIVE BY SCRIPTURE ALONE."

Don't limit yourself to only spiritual methods for coping or dealing with stress. Reading your scriptures and saying your prayers is essential—but so is taking a break. Sometimes the best cure for a bad day is a good meal, a competitive game of Uno, or laughing until you cry with your companion. Mission life is still life, and your soul is housed in a body that needs care. Draw something. Bake a cake. Play soccer on P-Day like it's the World Cup. The scriptures say that you should feel joy, so take time to find it in those little human experiences where it exists.

Ecclesiastes 3:1, 4

110

YOU WILL BAPTIZE MORE PEOPLE WITH YOUR LOVE THAN WITH YOUR LESSONS.

You might teach with clarity, bear testimony with conviction, and follow the lesson plan perfectly. But it's your love—your genuine, Christlike love—that people will remember. That's what opens hearts. That's what stays when the lessons have ended.

People may be introduced to the gospel through your words, but they'll stay because of how you made them feel. Don't just teach the message—be the message.

1 Corinthians 13:1–2

111

BE FLEXIBLE IN APPROACH, BUT FIRM IN CHARACTER.

Missionary work isn't one-size-fits-all. Every person you meet will respond to the Spirit differently, and the path to testimony may look different than you expect. Jesus taught in parables, through touch, with questions, and sometimes in silence. You're allowed to adapt. But there's a difference between flexibility and compromise. Never bend your values to avoid discomfort or to gain acceptance. You can change your schedule, your plan, or even your lesson approach—but never change your honesty, your covenants, or your core message.

John 10:14

112

NEVER USE THE WORD "TRUNKY" UNIRONICALLY.

If you're constantly counting down, you're missing the miracle of being here now. Counting down the days won't make them pass any faster, it will rob them of any joy.

Your mission is not a sentence to endure, it's a chapter to live.

Miracles happen in the *now*, not in the *next*. If you keep thinking about how long it is until you go home, you will miss the opportunities for learning and growth that the Lord puts right in front of you today.

Stay present. Stay faithful. Stay awake. If you have to modify your routine to create more joy and appreciation for the present day, do it.

Matthew 6:34

113
FINISH WHAT YOU START

One of the most underrated missionary skills is follow-through. It's easy to get excited at the beginning of a task, a project, or a commitment. But the real growth happens when you stay with it—even when it gets boring, difficult, or slow.

When you consistently finish what you start, you build trust with your companion, with members, with those you teach, and with the Lord. Half-effort brings half the results. Whole-hearted discipleship means doing what you said you'd do, even after the emotion of the moment fades. That's how integrity is born.

Ecclesiastes 7:8

114
ENDURE TO THE END.

Enduring to the end doesn't mean dragging yourself across the finish line with barely a testimony left. It means choosing every day—again and again—to love, to show up, to keep trying. Some days are miracles. Some feel like mud. But both are sacred in their own ways.

The end of your mission isn't just a calendar date—it's a culmination of thousands of quiet choices to believe, to forgive, to testify, to love, to keep going. Let Christ carry you on the hard days. He always finishes what He starts.

2 Nephi 31:20
2 Timothy 4:7

FINAL THOUGHTS

A mission is not just about what you accomplish, how many doors you knock, lessons you teach, or people you baptize. It's about how deeply you learn to love others. It's about the kind of disciple you choose to be when no one's watching. It's about letting the Savior write His story in your heart, one day, one conversation, one small act of courage at a time.

The lessons in this book are bigger than this book, and you will keep learning them throughout your life.

Some lessons will come through miracles. Others will come through heartbreak. Some will make sense right away while on your mission. Others won't until years later, when you're sitting in a church pew, or holding your first child, or comforting someone who feels lost. And suddenly, you'll realize—the mission never ended. It just changed shape.

So keep learning. Keep serving. Keep walking with the Savior. And wherever life takes you next, remember this: You were not just called on a mission. You were called to a way of life as a disciple of Christ.

Walk with Him and He will bless your life.

IN YOUR OWN WORDS

Use these blank pages to write down lessons you've learned from your mission that you could someday pass on to someone else. Your wisdom could one day strengthen another missionary who needs encouragement.

ABOUT THE AUTHOR

Dr. Kris Heap has spent years in church leadership, working closely with both youth and adults to strengthen faith, build resilience, and foster mean-
ingful discipleship. He brings a deep love for the gospel of Jesus Christ and a practical, compassionate approach to spiritual growth.

Through writing and public speaking, he has inspired countless individuals to find purpose in their challenges and to walk more intentionally with Christ. His writing is down-to-earth, encouraging, and focused on helping missionaries —past, present, and future—live with greater faith, perspective, and joy. For more information visit www.KrisHeap.com or scan the code below.

www.ingramcontent.com/pod-product-compliance
Lightning Source LLC
Chambersburg PA
CBHW050833010526
44110CB00054BA/2660